Central America and Panama

Central America and Panama

Patricia Maloney Markun

A FIRST BOOK | REVISED EDITION
FRANKLIN WATTS
NEW YORK | LONDON | TORONTO | SYDNEY | 1983

FRONTISPIECE: PRE-COLUMBIAN CERAMIC
FELINE-EFFIGY VESSEL FROM COSTA RICA

Map courtesy of Vantage Art, Inc.

Library of Congress Cataloging in Publication Data

Markun, Patricia Maloney.
Central America and Panama.

(A First book) Rev. ed. of:
The first book of Central America
and Panama. Rev. [2nd] ed. 1972.
Includes index.
Summary: A general introduction to the history,
geography, civilization, and industry of Central
America precedes descriptions of its seven countries.
1. Central America—Juvenile literature.
[1. Central America] I. Title.
F1428.5.M3 1983   972.8   82-20248
ISBN 0-531-04523-4

Contents

This edition is dedicated to the memory
of four North American women

Maura Clarke, Jean Donovan, Ita Ford,
and Dorothy Kazel

who were killed in El Salvador on
December 2, 1980

while working to improve the lives of
people in that troubled land

Central America and Panama

What the Land Is Like

Central America is an isthmus, a narrow spine of land connecting the two great landmasses of North and South America. The blue Pacific Ocean pounds on its west coast, eager to break through to the Caribbean Sea, beating on its east. As pictured on a map, the America to the north seems to be straining to get free from this slim land connection that ties it to the America of the south. The southern continent, meanwhile, appears to be swishing its Patagonian tail, trying to break away.

But the strip of Central American mountains stands firm, a dike between two oceans and a bridge between two continents. It refuses to sink into the sea. On the contrary, its lively volcanoes bubble and boil to build its spine higher. Every now and then one of the volcanoes breaks open and spews hot lava from the depths of the earth.

And very often an earthquake shakes the land somewhere along this Central American spine. The quake may be a mild trembling noticeable only on a seismograph, which records earth vibrations. The quake may be felt only by people in the upper story of a wooden house. Or it may be a violent moving of the earth such as

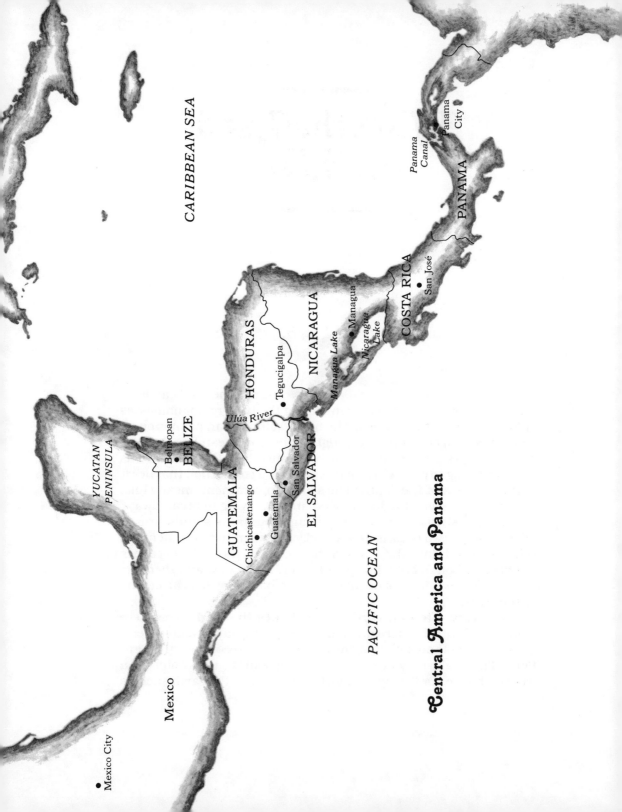

CARIBBEAN SEA

YUCATAN
PENINSULA

BELIZE
Belmopan ●

GUATEMALA

Chichicastenango ●
Guatemala ●
● San Salvador

EL SALVADOR

HONDURAS

Ulúa River

Tegucigalpa ●

NICARAGUA

Managua Lake
● Managua

*Nicaragua
Lake*

Panama
Canal

Panama
City ●

PANAMA

COSTA RICA

San José ●

Mexico

Mexico City ●

PACIFIC OCEAN

Central America and Panama

destroyed Guatemala's colonial capital in 1773 and heavily damaged its modern one first in 1918 and more recently in 1976.

Almost every afternoon, from about May through October, heavy rains pour down in many parts of Central America. These rainy months are called *invierno* (in-vee-AIR-no), or winter, in the Spanish language of the region. After the rainy period comes *verano* (ver-AHN-no), the summer of this two-season land. Then the sun shines steadily, and the same lands that lay muddy and soaked during the wet period shrivel up and crack in the desertlike climate of the dry season.

Central America is close to the equator, in a tropical latitude, but it is not all steaming, alligator country. The climate depends on the height of the land. Both of Central America's seacoasts are hot and humid. The people of the region call the sea-level land *tierra caliente* (tee-ERR-a cal-ee-EN-te), Spanish for "hot land." There are very few big cities in the uncomfortable seacoast areas.

Above 6,000 feet (1800 m) up in Central America's mountains, the climate is cold and the air thin. Here is the *tierra fria* (tee-ERR-a FREE-a), the "cold land," almost as unpopular a place to live in as the *tierra caliente*. While there is no permanent snow at this altitude, now and then a frost or a light flurry of snow causes great excitement among the mountain dwellers.

In Central America the ideal climate lies from about 2,000 to 6,000 feet (600 to 1800 m). This is the *tierra templada* (tee-ERR-a tem-PLAH-da), the "temperate land." The majority of Central America's people live at this altitude.

There are seven republics on the Central American isthmus: Guatemala, Honduras, El Salvador, Nicaragua, Costa Rica, Panama, and the new Republic of Belize, formerly British Honduras. All their capital cities are inland in the more temperate climate except Managua, in Nicaragua, and Panama City, on the Pacific coast of Panama. These cities grew up near sea level at points where coast-to-coast trails crossed between the mountains.

Generally, the Caribbean coast of Central America has much more moisture than the Pacific. The trade winds, blowing off the warm Caribbean, cool its coast and cause rain to fall there almost all the year round.

Central America Before Columbus

Thousands of years ago, it is thought, some of the peoples of Asia crossed the Bering Strait to what is now Alaska. From there they traveled slowly southward, seeking more sun and better hunting and fishing. Eventually, in hundreds of generations, a group of their descendants reached Central America. Some went even farther south to settle in South America, but others stayed to make their homes on the narrow, mountainous ridge between the oceans.

Wandering about in the two vastly empty continents, these earliest Americans made an important discovery. Somewhere they found corn, or maize, and learned to grow it. No one knows exactly where this plant was first used, or what it was like originally; one group of scientists thinks it may have been a grasslike weed discovered in the highlands of Central America. In any case, with cultivation it grew larger and more fruitful. As knowledge of it spread, it became the most important food for many Indian tribes throughout the Americas. Today the hillsides of Central America are green with the long-fingered leaves of growing corn, as they have been for hundreds and hundreds of years. Cornmeal, wrapped as dough around meat or some other filling to make

Indian families in villages of Central America
prepare tortillas in the traditional way.

tamales (ta-MAH-lees), or baked in round, thin cakes called *tortillas* (tor-TEE-yas), is still an important food in Central America.

Some of the early wanderers settled in the cool, springlike climate of the Guatemalan highlands. This beautiful region was the original home of Central America's highest pre-Spanish civilization—that of the Maya Indians.

Ruins of the Maya civilizations are still being found and studied by archaeologists in Guatemala, El Salvador, Honduras, and Belize in Central America, and also in Mexico. As scholars study their complex writing system, they are learning more of the history of this fascinating people. In the jungles and in the highlands, their elaborate temples and pyramids, as well as their palaces, have been discovered, sometimes covered by hundreds of years of growth of vines and bushes. Their amazing art—murals, pottery, stone sculpture—tells the story of a people with a highly creative culture.

From evidence found it seems that warfare and raiding were important in the lives of the Maya, although early archaeologists had thought them a completely peace-loving people. They were also successful farmers with huge reserves of food in their storehouses. They had well-built roads and traveled through Central and South America trading their woven cloth, pottery, feather work, and semiprecious stones.

The Maya were familiar with the rubber tree. Using a rubber ball, they played a complicated kind of basketball on a stone court. They grew, spun, and wove cotton. From the sapodilla tree they took the sap, or chicle, and used it for chewing gum. They made gold balls and other jewelry. They carved jade, sometimes in designs amazingly like those found in the Orient. (Is it a coincidence? Scientists wonder.)

On clear tropical nights the Maya studied the stars, and through the years their astronomers developed a calendar more accurate than the one used in Europe at the same time. So closely did they figure the journey of the earth around the sun that their time calculations were only two days off in figuring back over a period of 3,800 years. Over the same period the Europeans' Julian calendar strayed eleven days.

The Maya observed that the planet Venus took 584 days to orbit and achieve its selfsame former relationship with the earth and the sun. (The time is actually 583.9 days.) On the basis of this finding they developed a "Venus calendar" in addition to their solar calendar. To make up for the fraction of a day gained in their calculations, they dropped four days from their calendar every sixty-one years, thus making it accurate again.

At a time when Europe was using the clumsy Roman numeral system, the Maya had developed a better one. They based their system on twenty, rather than on ten as the Romans did, and their numbers were expressed by bars for five and dots for one. Independently and before any other people, they arrived at the idea of using a zero in mathematics—a great invention, indeed.

Concerning the Maya, there is one great mystery that archaeologists have not yet solved. Why did they leave their old empire in Guatemala? Between A.D. 800 and 900, six large lowland Maya centers were simply abandoned. The last dates carved into stone stelae (pillars) in all those sites fall within this one hundred-year period. Many of the people apparently moved from their well-watered lands north to the hot, dry Yucatán Peninsula in what is now Mexico. Evidence shows that they departed systematically, over a period of years. Making the change gradually as they did, they must have realized that they were moving to a place of poorer soil and less abundant water.

Some people have suggested that perhaps a terrible disease struck. Another guess is that severe earthquakes frightened the Indians and started the great migration. Overpopulation is another possibility. Estimates are that there were more than four hundred people per square mile in the original centers. Possibly they wore out the soil in their fields since they did not know about crop rotation or fertilization. When they needed new land, they simply burned a clearing in the forest and seeded it. Perhaps, when they had burned most of the trees away, grass overran the garden spots and could not be conquered with the poor digging sticks that were the people's only tools for cultivation. New land may have been necessary and may have prompted the Indians' migration.

Excavations continue at Tikal in northern Guatemala.
Eight huge pyramid-temples have been
uncovered in this great Maya city that
was buried under jungle for twelve centuries.

In any case, by A.D. 1000 a rich Maya civilization flourished in Yucatán, and the older centers were no longer important. Many of the ordinary farming Indians stayed in Guatemala, however, and in time moved back to their older homeland, the highlands.

By the time the Spanish landed in Central America, there were many different tribes of Indians, speaking several languages. In the Spaniards' bloody conquest of the land, they killed these Indians by the thousands. The tribes were scattered, their temples smashed. They became a conquered people, many of them the slaves of the Spanish invaders. But shreds of their customs and their culture still survive today, blended very often with those of the Spanish. In each of the republics of Central America, place names, folk legends, and dances recall the vanished Indian ancestors. There are two million Maya Indians today, speaking twenty-four different dialects.

In the Guatemalan highlands, especially, remnants of the old Indian ways live on. Among the misty volcanoes the descendants of the proud Maya pass on to their children the knowledge of their crafts: the weaving, the dances, and the music of their ancestors.

In the Republic of Panama, also, some tribes have resisted civilization. The Guaymi have retreated successfully to roadless mountain hideouts.

The Chocos and some Cunas live in the impenetrable jungle. To this day other Cunas have kept non-Indian people from settling on the thousand little islands of the San Blas Archipelago, off Panama's Caribbean coast. These Panama tribes still observe many ancient religious and tribal rites.

It is thought that the primitive Central American Indians may have done much trading with the Incas of Peru. Archaeologists from several universities in the Americas are digging at Central American sites and may find evidence that will link the local tribes more closely with those of South America.

The Spanish Conquer the Isthmus

Had Christopher Columbus gone a little farther westward on his fateful voyage in 1492, he would have come to what is now Central America. As it happened, another Spaniard, Rodrigo de Bastidas, sailing nine years later, in 1501, is credited with first sighting that land.

The year after, in 1502, Columbus on his last voyage arrived off the coast of what is now Honduras. Still looking for a westward passage, he turned his ships into one bay after another along Central America's Caribbean coast as his hopes faded. Shipworms were burrowing into the hulls of his vessels, and his crews were mutinous, impatient to return to Spain. In 1504, off the coast of Panama, he gave up. He ordered his ships to sail for home. Two years later he died in Spain without ever finding the "great ocean to the west," which the Indians had told him was near. He was never to know that Central America was a narrow isthmus, providing a solid wall against sailing west to reach the Pacific.

The first white man to sight the "western sea" was Vasco Núñez de Balboa, in 1513. Setting out across the isthmus in what is now Panama, he sighted the Pacific Ocean from a high peak and proceeded to the shore, claiming for Spain the sea and all the land it touched.

Soon afterward the Spanish subdued the Indians in the western part of Panama, but the chief conquest of Central America came from the north.

Hernán Cortés had taken Mexico for Spain, and in 1523 he selected one of his men to overcome the Indians of the region farther south. His choice as conqueror was one of his bravest, most handsome officers, the red-haired Pedro de Alvarado. The Maya Indians called him Tonatiuh, "Child of the Sun."

Once he had succeeded in conquering the natives, Alvarado was in charge of a region governed under the Spanish crown and known as the Kingdom of Guatemala. It extended from Mexico southward through Costa Rica. This Spanish colonial leader organized it into eight provinces: Chiapas, Yucatán, Guatemala, Verapaz, El Salvador, Nicaragua, Honduras, and Costa Rica. Surprisingly, these regions carry the same names today. Chiapas and Yucatán are now parts of Mexico, and Verapaz is included in Guatemala. The other five of Alvarado's provinces are now independent republics.

Under the Spanish crown each of Alvarado's provinces had its own strong local government, headed by a powerful governor. Each governor was responsible to the Spanish king's representative in Guatemala. The high mountains discouraged communication among the different regions, rendering each province independent to a certain extent.

Panama, which had been conquered from the south, was not part of the Kingdom of Guatemala. Its main traffic was with Peru, and it became part of that Spanish region in 1542. Later it was joined to New Granada, and still later to Colombia. And so, although Panama is a part of Central America in its geography, in its history it has not truly been so.

Belize was settled by the British in the 1600s on land that Spain claimed but did not occupy. After the Central American republics were formed, Guatemala long continued to claim Belize, but the British never allowed the claim.

How the Republics Were Formed

The Spanish came to America chiefly as conquerors. Their ambition was to take as much land or find as much gold as they could, then go back to Spain to live on the profits. Rarely did they bring their wives and children with them. "To the victor belong the spoils" was the rule in most of Central America. As a result, huge tracts of land went to each Spanish officer who had helped Alvarado, Cortés, and the other leaders.

Local rule by a tyrannical Spanish governor kept the native Central Americans from learning democratic self-government. The Spanish governor, supported by a few rich landowners loyal to the crown, was in absolute control; no middle class was allowed to develop. When some of the descendants of the original Spanish officers eventually came to live on their inherited estates, their sons were sent back to Spain to be educated. These young men married the daughters of other well-to-do landholders. The landlords were often absent from their huge holdings and were interested only in profits. The majority of the people were barefoot laborers (peons) who went through life with no chance to own a piece of land or to learn to read or write.

Early in the nineteenth century, Simón Bolívar, the great liberator, stirred South Americans to revolt against Spanish rule. The fever for independence spread to Mexico and from there went southward through Central America. On September 15, 1821, the Central Americans, following in the steps of the rebelling Mexicans, issued the Declaration of Independence of Central America. The revolt was successful; the representatives of the Spanish crown departed.

For two years thereafter Central America was a part of the new Mexican republic. Then the five territories of Guatemala, El Salvador, Honduras, Nicaragua, and Costa Rica formed the United Provinces of Central America. In 1826 they adopted a constitution patterned after that of the United States.

But from the beginning the government was shaky. High mountain walls separated the provinces and made it hard for them to communicate with one another. As a result, they had no understanding of one another's thoughts and problems. In addition, for nearly three hundred years each section had been accustomed to the rule of a powerful Spanish governor. Now the provinces found it difficult to unite. In 1838 the federation was dissolved, and each member became an independent republic.

One small part of the isthmus was not included in the five republics—the northernmost Atlantic coast area of Central America. Probably settled by shipwrecked British sailors around 1638, it was part of Jamaica until 1884, when it became the crown colony of British Honduras. Its chief value to Britain was its excellent mahogany lumber, which British shipbuilders prized. According to a story, one of Sir Walter Raleigh's vessels, riddled by shipworms, had stopped on the coast of British Honduras for repairs. When mahogany planks were substituted for the worm-eaten ones, the British discovered that the new lumber was worm resistant. Later the famous English furniture makers, Sheraton, Hepplewhite, and Chippendale, discovered its beautiful grain; this wonderful wood, strong and hard, could be carved into graceful, delicate shapes.

Descendants of the Carib Indians and African slaves settled in the tiny jungle-covered country. But aside from its lumber mills, British Honduras developed little industry. The country, now called Belize, broke its last colonial ties with Great Britain in 1981.

As to Panama, in 1903—on the third try—it staged a successful revolution and gained its independence from Colombia. The new republic at once signed a treaty with the United States, creating the Canal Zone. In exchange for a guarantee of its independence and an annually paid sum of money, Panama granted to the United States a strip of land 10 miles (16 km) wide for the construction, maintenance, and sanitation of a canal between the Caribbean Sea and Pacific Ocean. The grant gave the United States the right to govern the zone and was to last "in perpetuity"—forever. Later treaties, adopted in 1979, abolished the Canal Zone, set up a U.S. military zone around the Panama Canal, and turned over much land to Panama.

One by one the new republics adopted constitutions similar to that of the United States. In each of the constitutions, provision was made for a president and an elected congress. It was not long, however, before a "strong man," or dictator, set himself up in nearly all the new nations.

At various times nearly all the republics of the Central American isthmus have had revolutions and shaky governments. In some of the countries, a president rarely completes his term of office. Panama, for example, in 78 years has had more presidents than the United States has had in over 192 years.

Where there is little faith in the government, businesses are afraid to invest money to build up the country. Long-term works such as roads and hydroelectric plants are hard to complete; before they are finished a new government with different ideas has taken over. The original project often stands uncompleted; the money has been entirely wasted. Stable, democratic government is one of the most important needs of Central America.

In most of the countries, some rich families, descendants of the sixteenth-century Spaniards, still have large landholdings. Thousands of landless, penniless peons work for the few wealthy families of property. How to break up the huge estates so that more people may own land and how to train them to use the land wisely are big problems.

*The Thatcher Ferry Bridge, at the Pacific
entrance to the Panama Canal, unites the Americas.*

Billions of dollars in United States money has been spent since World War II to try to improve the agricultural economy of Central America and Panama. U.S. financed plans included the Marshall Plan's Point Four programs and the Alliance for Progress' AID programs.

High-salaried American technicians—experts in developing seed corn, breeding cattle, growing rice, and developing export crops like tomatoes—have spent a total of thousands of work years in these countries. Their children have grown up in Central American capital cities while the families lived there at U.S. government expense.

In addition, since the early 1960s, through the Peace Corps hundreds of enthusiastic, though inexperienced, young people have worked in Central America, many of them trying to improve agriculture. Other serious efforts have been made over a number of years by IBEC, sponsored by the Rockefeller Foundation.

Yet, after more than forty years of American effort and aid, both public and private, the plight of the poor farmers, the *campesinos* (kahm-pay-SEE-nos), is no better in many places.

Stories of small successes in improving agriculture with American assistance have come out of Central America from time to time. Projects sponsored by local progressive Catholic bishops in combination with U.S. aid or other help have been successful, at least briefly.

Overall, however, the successful combination of the poor farmers willing to make changes; the needed aid at the right time; knowledge of local climate, markets, crops, and diseases; and long-range cooperation of the government has been rare. Great efforts have produced surprisingly few successes from tremendous years of service, a huge amount of money, and the combined work and hopes of Central Americans and U.S. supporters.

Scattered through these seven countries are the remains of projects begun with U.S. money and enthusiasm that did not succeed. Rice-drying plants have been built that did not work or were completed too late to be useful. Ambitious experimental planting programs have taken place at tremendous expense to show Central Americans how to grow such new crops as rubber trees, mahogany trees, tomatoes, rice, and cotton. Enthusiasm died once the funding gave out, and local farmers failed to carry out the new ideas.

New and higher-producing strains of corn, the area's basic crop, have been introduced, but few farmers continue to grow the newer varieties.

U.S. standards and practices in cattle raising have been successfully adopted in many places. These have resulted in superior breeds of cattle that produce more milk and better beef and that withstand tropical heat and diseases better. Yet, by and large, these changes work for the benefit of the wealthy cattle-ranch owner. The poor *campesinos* cannot afford cattle, very often not even one cow.

As the revolution of Communist Fidel Castro succeeded in the 1960s and 1970s on the nearby island of Cuba, its influence was sure to touch the whole Caribbean basin. Millions of poor, uneducated Central Americans have had little hope of a better life under the rule of a rich minority. Understandably, they listen to Cubans who spread revolutionary teachings.

The Banana in Central America

Any account of Central America must include the story of the banana, which has played an important part in the region's development.

Unlike corn and cacao, which were first found in the New World, the banana was imported. In 1516 a few roots were brought to the island of Hispaniola (now Haiti and the Dominican Republic) from the Canary Islands by Friar Tomás de Berlanga, then bishop of Panama. The transplanted roots flourished, and the banana spread through Central America and the Caribbean area.

In the time of the clipper ships, New England sea captains on occasional trips to Central and South America brought home the strange yellow fruit. Just after the Civil War the first commercial shipment of bananas arrived in New York from plantations near the present Panama Canal. The fruit was still rare enough in 1876, however, to cause a sensation at the Philadelphia Centennial Exposition. There bananas, each carefully wrapped in tinfoil, were sold at a fabulous price.

No one could have predicted that they would become so important a product. The United Fruit Company, the biggest banana producer of them all, began as a sideline to something else. Minor Keith, one of the founders, was an engineer who had built a railroad in Costa Rica. Experimenting also with a banana plantation, he found the fruit an unbelievably profitable freight for his new transportation system; in fact, it was the financial lifesaver of the railroad.

Soon he realized that there might be more money in bananas than in railroads, and he planted the Costa Rican valleys with the fruit. In 1899 he joined his property with that of the Boston Fruit Company to form the United Fruit Company. A few years later, in order to transport bananas, the company chartered the freight ship *Venus*. Someone thought of fitting it with refrigeration equipment to keep the easily spoiled bananas cool in their journey through the tropical heat to North America. Thus began a great step forward in ocean transportation. Today refrigerated ships, first developed to carry bananas, are commonplace for perishable cargoes all over the world.

In President Theodore Roosevelt's time the banana business grew fast. One by one, Guatemala, Honduras, Nicaragua, Costa Rica, and Panama signed agreements with the fruit companies. Huge tracts of hot, moist lowlands were granted to the banana growers—lands that were swampy, roadless, and unused. In exchange the fruit companies were to build railroads and develop port facilities. At that time nearly every port in Central America was a fever-ridden pesthole. The harbors were dredged, and then docks were built by the fruit growers.

Since the native Central Americans have always preferred to live and work in the highlands, the banana companies brought in laborers—the Negroes of Jamaica, Martinique, Barbados, and other Caribbean islands—who did not mind the hot, sea-level climates. Tall and muscular, they could do much more demanding physical labor than could the more slightly built, shorter Spanish-Indian Central American natives.

Banana raising has always been a risky business. Earth-

*Using assembly-line techniques, these packers
prepare bananas for export by refrigerated ships.*

quakes and volcanic eruptions, as well as floods and blowdowns by strong winds, must be expected in the Central American countries. Since the entire fruit crop may be wiped out in one area, the growers must plan to have more than one plantation. Thereby, losses in one place may be regained by profits in another. In addition, various plant diseases must be overcome by scientific research and the introduction of disease-resistant types of the fruit.

Commercial banana growing has become a complicated science. A system of land flooding brings deep layers of rich soil from the rivers to the plantations. Careful pruning preserves the high quality of bananas. Irrigation is used, and ditches must be dug and maintained. The surrounding lush growth must be kept cleaned away until the young banana stalks are tall enough to provide shade to discourage other plants. They must be sprayed to prevent insects and leaf diseases.

From ten months to a year after planting, each stalk yields a stem (bunch) of fruit weighing from 75 to 100 pounds (33.75 to 45 kg). Because the banana is a giant herb, not a tree, its stalk is not a woody growth. Each plant produces but a single stem of fruit, and after this is harvested, the plant is cut down.

The big fruit companies have worked out a time schedule for growing bananas. Keeping in mind the needs of consumers in the United States, they know exactly when to cut a stem and how long to allow for hauling it to a ship for loading. They figure a certain number of days for transportation to a particular port in the United States, then to a certain market. The arrival of the golden yellow bananas you bought at the fruit counter the other afternoon was timed almost to the day. It is hard to realize that the fruit was hard and green that moist, hot morning when it was picked in Central America weeks before.

In recent years there has been a boom in the banana market. More Europeans are buying bananas, and sales of bananas in the United States have also increased.

The fruit growers have turned Central America's fever-filled swamps into lush, productive farms. Orderly rows of properly fertilized banana plants spread like green, living stripes across the

*Workers lay irrigation pipes
on a banana plantation in Honduras.*

lowlands. To help accomplish this, the growers have built workers' towns. The United States' practices in sanitation and agriculture have made many areas of the Central American lowlands liv-
able. The fruit companies provide safe drinking water. They pay
higher wages to their thousands of employees than do native
employers. They run a system of schools for employees' children.
They maintain hospitals partly staffed with physicians who have
been trained in the United States. In each country they have built
churches for their workers. They maintain company commissar-
ies so that employees can buy food, clothing, and other essentials
cheaply.

In 1912, a strange root disease struck the banana plantations
of Central America. Because it first showed up in Panama, it was
named the Panama disease. From then on, the fruit companies
frequently moved their plantations. Land on which the disease
had attacked was allowed to remain fallow for several years. Then
another crop would be planted of the Gros Michel—the "big
Mike"—the variety of banana that had proved to be the biggest
and best for shipping to market in other countries. The only way to
keep ahead of the Panama disease was to keep moving.

In 1958, after much experimentation, United Fruit began to
raise the Valery or Cavendish strain of banana. One of its great
advantages was that it was immune to the Panama disease. No
longer did the fruit companies need to allow land to remain fallow.
They returned lands to the countries in which they operated. In
Panama they gave back all the land they had held for a half century and now just rent what they need from the government. In
Honduras they gave back the land as well as a railroad (now government owned and run) and the manager's large home (now operated as a resort by the government).

Charges are made from time to time that the fruit companies
in the past have tried to influence the governments in Latin America. The policy of one large company, United Brands, now is to
make a special effort "to be a good guest" in the lands in which
they operate. The few non-native employees in the companies are
each encouraged to "be a good guest" and to use that as a stan-
dard for behavior abroad.

Take a train, board a ship in a port, send a cable, or place a telephone call in Central America, and chances are that the fruit companies first developed that facility. The restoration of the Mayan city of Zaculeu in Guatemala was a long-term endeavor of one of the fruit companies. So was the development of the fine Museum of Archaeology in San José, Costa Rica, and the Agricultural School at Zamorano, in Honduras.

As the Central American countries have become more aware of themselves as nations, they have developed a resentment toward the northern ownership of the banana companies. This is particularly so where strong labor unions have been organized among banana workers. Fruit growers are accused of grabbing great chunks of land.

It is understandable that the Central American republics should wish to control their own industries. One company has found an answer to the problem of the fruit business by leasing or selling its land to individual native growers. While the Central Americans run the property, the fruit company supplies know-how and promises to buy the bananas. In this way the Central Americans are learning to run the plantations themselves.

The Seven Republics

Strung out along the isthmus, between the two seas, lie the seven republics. Their people—walled in by mountains, often cut off by poor roads, and clinging to the isolated highlands in order to avoid as far as possible the hot, unhealthful seacoasts—have tended to stay within their own borders.

So, small as the republics are, each of them has developed its own individual character.

It is only recently that the completion of the Inter-American Highway and political unrest have combined to end this isolation. Refugees moved from Nicaragua to Costa Rica during the Nicaraguan civil war. Because of fighting in El Salvador, numbers of people have fled over the border to Honduras. A far greater number—estimated in millions—have gone by bus and truck up the Inter-American Highway.

Illegally, they have found their way into Mexico, and thousands have gone even farther north to cross the border into the United States as illegal aliens.

GUATEMALA

There is a magic to Guatemala. Visitors have come back to it again and again. They would fall in love with its blue, blue sky and the splendor of its many volcanoes, pushing their cones heavenward. They were enchanted by the mysterious mountain mists and the colorful Indians and their villages. Because of the cool, crisp climate of its highlands, Guatemala is often called "the land of eternal spring."

Located just south of Mexico, it is the northernmost Central American republic. Although it is only the third largest in area, it has the biggest population, estimated at over six million, and it has more pure Indians than any other Central American country. More than half of its people are descended from the Maya or other tribes, while the remainder are largely *ladinos* (lah-DEE-nos), people of mixed Spanish and Indian ancestry.

Although Spanish is the official language of the country, in many Indian towns high in the mountains the people still speak only their native Indian tongue. Each area has its distinctive costume. The color of the skirt and the pattern of woven decoration vary from village to village and so identify the people of each place. There are 345 different village costumes in Guatemala.

The women and little girls wear long skirts, *refajos* (re-FAH-yos), topped by gay blouses called *huipiles* (hwee-PEE-les) and fringed shawls called *perrajes* (per-RAH-yez). The boys from a particular town can be recognized by these same fringed shawls and by the embroidery on their trousers. The men's coats are usually short and stiff; their trousers are either long or short, and slit woolen trousers resembling Scottish kilts are often worn over cotton ones.

Chichicastenango is probably the most interesting Indian village in the country. It is famous for the weekly fair held in its tiny

Sunday market in the central square of Chichicastenango

central square, for its religious festivals, and for the crowds wearing the colorful dress typical of each village. Many of the Indians of the surrounding countryside attend mass in its local Catholic church, but because of a great shortage of priests, they have had little instruction in the Catholic religion. Outside, on the church steps overlooking the square, they burn incense to their ancient gods and kneel in prayer. The women weave the costumes of cotton on portable looms, which they tie at one end around their waists and at the other up to a tree, an overhanging roof, or some other high place. In highland villages where the climate is cold, the women and girls weave heavier cloth than in hot, lowland places where lighter cloth is more comfortable.

The capital of the country, Guatemala City, lies in the midst of the west-central highlands where most of the Guatemalans live. With more than 1,500,000 inhabitants, it is the biggest city in Central America. Its huge market features flowers and handicrafts from all over the country. The city and much of the *altiplano* (ahl-te-PLAH-no) are still recovering from the disastrous earthquake of 1976 in which 25,000 people were killed and thousands of buildings destroyed.

About an hour's ride away by automobile is Antigua, the ancient capital—then known as Santiago—dating back to the days of Alvarado, governor of the kingdom. He set out to create a beautiful capital city for Guatemala. When the volcano Fuego erupted in 1541, the site at Ciudad Vieja was covered by mud. Another place was chosen, a magnificent spot in the mountain valley of Panchoy. Architects and builders came from Spain to design a cathedral, convents and monasteries, plazas, and government buildings.

Hundreds of the newly vanquished Maya Indians were sought out by the Spanish to build Santiago, the city of beauty. Among them were expert stonemasons, who had learned their craft in building temples before their conquerors arrived. Even an aqueduct was constructed to bring water from the mountains. A city of magnificent buildings arose. The Palace of the Captains General was perhaps the most impressive of all, with rows and rows of majestic pillars and arches.

The capital grew remarkably in the next two hundred years. By 1773 it had a population of nearly 70,000. There were fifty-seven churches and eight colleges, including the University of San Carlos. Then, one day in that year, an earthquake shook the city to its foundations. Hastily gathering up what few possessions they could carry, the inhabitants fled the swaying, quivering buildings and streamed in terror through the mountains.

A new site was chosen for the center of government, and the old capital was completely abandoned. Referred to as "Antigua" (Spanish for "old"), it lay almost forgotten for more than a hundred years. Finally, investigators discovered that the solidly constructed buildings were not so severely damaged as had been thought. Cleaned, rebuilt where necessary, and reoccupied, the buildings of Antigua lie peacefully in the hills of Guatemala, undisturbed by modern bustle. One of the abandoned ancient monasteries has been made into a hotel, and several of the old homes have been reoccupied. The buildings of pastel shades—pink or yellow—are charming. Walking through Antigua, a person can easily pretend to be living two hundred years ago, with Spain still the master of Central America and Antigua the proudest capital of the New World.

The lakes of Guatemala are beautiful. Amatitlán, bounded by mountains and wooded hills, is used for waterskiing and for swimming and boating. Skin divers have brought up from its bottom many relics of the Mayan villages that formerly clustered around its shores.

Lake Atitlán lies farther up in the highlands, steeply surrounded by mountains, four of which are volcanoes. Perched on its shores are a dozen little Indian villages, named for one each of the twelve apostles. Indians in dugout canoes paddle from village to village over the unfathomably deep waters of the lake, and an air of mystery and remoteness hovers over all. Here is truly the Guatemala of the Indians.

In the north of the country lie the hot lowland forests of Petén, which makes up about one-third of Guatemala. Much of the land is so wild and hard to reach that it is of little practical use.

In Petén also—at Uaxactún, Tikal, and other sites—some of

the most impressive of the ancient Maya ruins have been found. And the forests may hide many more, awaiting discovery.

Guatemala, its soil enriched by volcanic lava, is primarily an agricultural country. Its chief export crop is coffee, whose mildness and flavor make it a favorite for blending with other varieties. The coffee trees grow best at from 1,000 to 5,000 feet (300 to 1,500 m) above sea level, and the climate of the west-central highlands is ideal for them. The recent drop in coffee prices worldwide has meant less income from that crop in sales to other countries.

Although Guatemalan Indian weaving is a fine art, it is now also done commercially. Quezaltenango is the textile center; there striking materials for skirts and dresses are woven, embroidered, and sold to declining numbers of tourists or exported to many parts of the world.

The warm Pacific lowlands, with their rich soil, are the principal cotton-growing area. Cotton is used in the native weaving industry and in recent years has been produced in surplus, for export. Since cotton is important as a crop, researchers have been working to find the types best suited to the climate, growing dozens of varieties experimentally. Other Guatemalan exports are beef and bananas.

An important new development in Guatemala is the discovery of oil. It is too early to tell what changes this will bring to the economy, but in 1981 it was expected that up to one million barrels would be produced by five oil wells in that year.

Although two-thirds of the country's electricity has until recently been produced by thermal sources, two large hydroelectric projects are being completed in Aguacapa and Chixoy. A third dam, bigger than both of those together, is expected to be constructed at Chulas by the late 1980s.

Indian women today still weave
richly patterned fabrics
on old-style, back-strap looms.

Guatemala is a country that tourists have long enjoyed visiting. However, the recent political disturbances in Central America and terrorist incidents in Guatemala have greatly discouraged the tourist business.

Guatemala has had a long, troubled political history. In the past forty years, violence has increased as opposing military officers struggle to control the government. Generals and colonels have been elected for terms as president that they rarely complete before another governmental upset.

New constitutions have been introduced and have been suspended, then replaced. Leftist guerrillas and rightist vigilantes known as "death squads" have tried to stop the violence, only to produce more of it. Many unsolved murders and assassinations of foreign diplomats, such as the ambassador of the United States to Guatemala, have taken place.

The presidential elections in March 1982 brought about a coup by an unsuccessful group of officers who charged that the elections had not been honest. The general who was within months of completing a four-year term as president was ousted. A junta (HOON-tah) led by a retired general took power and promised that another election would soon be held.

At the present time, the upper 2 percent of the Guatemalans enjoy one-fourth of the country's income. The lower one-half of the country's population gets only 10 to 15 percent of income. The government has begun land reform, cutting up the huge plantations owned by the rich to give the rural poor their own land to farm.

Guatemala was active in the Central America Common Market (CACM). The social revolutions taking place in El Salvador and Nicaragua have disrupted the trade in the CACM, to which much of Guatemala's exports in recent years used to flow.

Education is one of the biggest problems facing Guatemala, more than half of whose people are illiterate. There are so few schools that only one-third of the children are able to attend. There is a school for training teachers for the rural areas, where the need is greatest. The University of San Carlos in Guatemala City has law and medical schools in addition to many other courses. There is a national school of nursing and a people's university for the encouragement of adult education. Development of a country depends on the literacy of its people. Although education or development does not guarantee democratic government, people who have no education are easier to oppress.

HONDURAS

The Republic of Honduras is a country the size of Ohio, wedged into the mountains between its more powerful neighbors, Guatemala and Nicaragua. El Salvador lies to the southwest and the Caribbean Sea to the north. The country is mountainous almost everywhere, yet Honduras is the one Central American republic with no volcanoes.

Through the center of the country, between the mountains, runs the broad plain of Comayagua. From it, one river, the Ulua, goes north to the Caribbean. Another, the Goascarán, flows south to the Pacific. The plain and the two river valleys together form a depression that crosses the entire country.

Soon after its discovery, this area was pointed out as an excellent place for a canal across the isthmus. Later it was hoped that the first interoceanic railroad might be built across this lowland region. But Honduras has had a stormy political history, and partly because of lack of steady leadership, it has never achieved either the ocean-to-ocean railroad or the canal.

It is the least developed of the Central American countries. Its annual per capita income in 1981 was $565, the second lowest in the Western Hemisphere.

On the country's Caribbean coast there are some railroads, built to serve the tremendous banana plantations that run through the lowlands. Boats transport people up some of the eleven navigable rivers. Many little airstrips, cut along the riverbanks and in the jungles, lie like patchwork across Honduras. Light airplanes use them, landing and taking off, to carry travelers over the impenetrable mountain forests. Planes help make up for the shortage of good roads for land transportation.

Honduras is a real banana country. Raising and exporting the fruit is the biggest national industry and it has been said that "bananas shake the Honduran economic tree." Coffee growing and exporting are very important to the Honduran economy, and growth in the cattle industry has made beef export a major activity. Strong labor unions have developed among the Honduran banana workers that have brought them many benefits.

One of the United Fruit Company's great contributions to Central America is the Pan American School of Agriculture at Zamorano, about twenty-four miles from Tegucigalpa. Here the newest techniques in tropical agriculture are taught young men who are scholarship students from a number of Latin American republics. Their training is carefully planned so that on returning home they may be of use to the agriculture of their particular country. All students are required not only to study from books but to do actual work with their hands: planting, cultivating, and harvesting.

There has been a feeling among some upper-class Latin Americans that there is no dignity in physical labor. The school is trying to overcome this prejudice, as is necessary if Latin America is to progress. Instructors at the school are graduates of agricultural colleges, who teach students the pride of all work connected with agriculture.

In Honduras there are about 3,500,000 people, most of them a mixture of Spanish and Indian. The majority still live scattered about the country as poor farmers, tilling small plots of ground or working on the estates of wealthy landowners. The houses of the countryside and villages are humble, made of adobe (mud brick) with tiled roofs.

Less than half the population can read and write, but 70 percent of the children go to school to learn how. Living for the farming people is simple and often difficult. In the banana regions, workers may live in company-built homes and in towns planned by the fruit growers.

The program at the Pan American School
of Agriculture combines practical
fieldwork with academic studies.

Because land transportation routes are poor, Hondurans have a hard time reaching one another, let alone the outside world. Yet they have long favored the union of the countries of Central America. Their greatest hero is Francisco Morazán, the plumed-hatted, high-booted president of the short-lived United Provinces of Central America (1823–1838). The Honduran flag still carries five stars, signifying the five Central American states of the United Provinces.

The earliest capital of Honduras was Comayagua, on the river of the same name. In 1632 the first university in Central America was founded in this city. Comayagua's cathedral, with its beautiful colonial architecture, is one of the finest buildings in Central America and has a painting, "The Martyrdom of Saint Bartholomew," by the Spanish painter Murillo.

Tegucigalpa's location in the mountains near rich silver mines has made it the leading city of Honduras. Even today silver, as well as the minerals lead and zinc, is exported.

After Central American independence from Spain, the seat of government alternated between Comayagua and Tegucigalpa until 1880. In that year, Tegucigalpa became the permanent capital. Some years later the smaller city of Comayagüela, on the other side of the Choluteca River, was incorporated with it. Together, the two cities are now known as the Central District, and seven bridges link them.

Like all Central American capitals, "Teguc," as it is nicknamed, has its central square. It is called Parque Morazán for the man who attempted Central American union. The cathedral, the Palace of the Central District, and the National Museum face the square. The Presidential Palace is a beautiful building located on the Choluteca River. Across the stream in the Comayagüela section are the National University and the National School of Fine Arts.

This carved stela from a plaza at Copán may be a portrait of a noblewoman.

Tegucigalpa, with a population of 450,000, is the only capital in Central America not located on the Inter-American Highway, although an all-weather spur road does link the highway with the city.

The highway passes through the Pacific port of San Lorenzo, a port that is useful now only at high tide. The increased traffic of the new road may bring more commerce to San Lorenzo and also to Choluteca, in the lumbering region through which the highway passes. Much of the Honduran mahogany, famous for generations, is cut in the sawmills of Choluteca.

Near the Guatemalan border is one of the greatest attractions of Honduras: the fabulous city of Copán, abandoned by the Maya thirteen hundred years ago. Its ruins are beautiful and impressive. Ball courts, temples, altars, palaces, sunken courtyards, pyramids, and a large stadium suggest something of the life of the ancient people. A great plaza is marked with stelae, sculptured pillars of stone, which were raised every ten or twenty years to commemorate important dates and events. A huge stairway is decorated with strange carvings. Harvard University and the Carnegie Institution have spent thousands of dollars in unearthing Copán. From it archaeologists are constantly trying to piece together more of the intriguing history of the Maya.

EL SALVADOR

Tucked in under the shoulders of Guatemala and Honduras is El Salvador, whose name means "the Savior" in Spanish. Bordering on the Pacific, it is the only Central American republic that does not also have a Caribbean coastline. Although it is the smallest of the original Central American countries, it is also the most densely populated. In 1981 it was estimated to have 4,805,000 people, of whom the greater number are of Indian or mixed Indian and Spanish blood.

In this small country of hills, mountains, and upland plains there are twenty-two volcanoes. No matter where a person goes in El Salvador, a volcano is almost always in view.

In many parts of the country, hot mud pools boil and geyser-like jets of steam rush from the ground, showing evidence of volcanic activity beneath the earth's surface. There are springs of mineral waters, and the volcanoes have turned up soils of almost every color.

The capital of the country is San Salvador, a city of more than 400,000 people. It lies in a broad valley that has been swayed and moved by so many earthquakes that it is called the Valley of Hammocks. Its residents are used to earthquakes and make their buildings low and solid to withstand them as far as possible.

The city, also named after the Holy Savior, is roughly laid out in the form of a cross. Its oldest church, La Merced, has a historic bell that first became famous in 1811. That was the year in which Father José Matías Delgado rang the bell to announce a revolt against Spanish rule. Although his revolution failed, he is now honored as the national hero.

The government administration buildings, the National University, and a big public market are all located in the capital. Flowers brighten the city, and the Campo de Marte, its largest park, is a scenic spot. The highest peak of the surrounding mountains is also named San Salvador. It looks down protectingly on the city.

Just 9 miles (14.4 km) away is Lake Ilopango, whose waters fill an ancient volcanic crater. It is surrounded by resort hotels as well as by older Indian fishing villages.

The coffee blossom is El Salvador's national flower—and with reason, for coffee is by far the country's largest and most important crop. The mountain slopes and the rich volcanic soil make this an ideal coffee-raising region. More than half of El Salvador's total exports are coffee.

Unfortunately for the majority of the people, the profits of the tremendous coffee harvest have in the past been controlled by a small number of very rich families. El Salvador was colonized by *catorce familias* (kah-TOR-say fah-MEE-lee-us), fourteen families that for three hundred years owned most of the farmland and the largest part of the wealth of the country. The original fourteen families grew to a few hundred over the years, but in the late

1970s that 2 percent of the people owned 60 percent of all the farmlands in the country. The few very wealthy families lived in beautiful mansions in San Salvador, many in marble palaces in the suburb of San Benito, while hundreds of hungry children begged in the streets of the city.

Coffee prices fell in the late 1970s, and the lot of the poor landless peasants working for the landowners became even worse off. Revolutionaries who had been successful in the nearby land of Nicaragua helped to create greater unrest.

Violence and revolution erupted, and, in January 1980, the Christian Democratic Party announced that it would form a new government. It also announced the Basic Law of Land Reform. It was the first step in transferring ownership of half the country's property to peasant cooperatives and to individual tenant farmers.

For the first time ever, thousands of people who had no land, or hopes of owning land, could now have the hope of owning part of a formerly large plantation and farming it.

Landless peasants were to be able to acquire as much as 17 acres (6.8 ha) of land that they themselves were cultivating. To strengthen small business and to make credit available for land reform, the government took over the partial ownership of the country's banks.

However, the country's military force opposed the new moves, and terrorist activity increased. Hundreds of people were killed in seemingly senseless shooting episodes, as opposing groups sought to take over the government. A number of Catholic priests who spoke out about injustice were murdered. Archbishop Oscar Romero, leader of the church in San Salvador, was shot and killed while saying mass in the city's cathedral in March 1980. At his

Sacks of coffee beans,
El Salvador's largest export,
are loaded on cargo ships in
the modern port of Acajutla.

funeral in the same cathedral, violence broke out and several people died.

Eight months later four Americans—three American nuns and a woman social worker—were kidnapped and killed. The next month two visiting American labor union specialists were assassinated along with the head of El Salvador's land reform institution, whom the Americans had come to advise.

Bands of guerrillas have bombed stores, burned crops, and murdered business people in an effort to wreck the country's economy. The guerrillas remain entrenched in isolated parts of Morazán and Chalatenango provinces near the Honduran border. In this way they have access to help from other countries by way of Honduras. Many refugees from El Salvador are living in camps in Honduras.

Elections were held in March 1982 in which 70 percent of the country's voters took part, in spite of threats from the guerrillas, who tried to discourage people from voting. The Christian Democrats, led by José Napoleón Duarte, got 40 percent of the votes. However, when the country's Assembly (similar to the U.S. Congress) met, candidates of the other parties voted together and outnumbered the Christian Democrats. As a result, the majority of votes went to Roberto d'Aubuisson, who became Constituent Assembly President.

With d'Aubuisson as the country's leader, some feared that land reforms started by Duarte could slow down or stop. In the past d'Aubuisson had been opposed both to land reform and to human rights.

In 1981, the U.S. Congress pledged to reduce military and economic aid to El Salvador if the land reform program did not go ahead and if human rights progress stopped. Four months after the election the United States' ambassador to El Salvador reported that the newly elected government was continuing Duarte's land-reform practices and was showing concern for human rights.

By July of 1982, a total of 30,000 *campesinos* (farmers) had become landowners since the onset of the land-reform program. In the human rights arena, plans were underway to hold trials for a number of soldiers suspected of murdering the four American woman missionaries.

After the election, there was a reduction in the level of violence. For the first time, there were signs of institutional change. For example, a new Supreme Court was named. Military force personnel were apprehended for crimes and were punished.

Just after the election, some tried to destroy the land reform that Duarte had begun earlier. However, now the army is helping to reinstate the *campesinos* who had been temporarily ousted. The government is now paying compensation to those whose lands have been given to others.

Because of the poverty and lack of an equal chance for most of the people, this beautiful, green-ridged land is a center of political unrest. There is little opportunity for most of the Salvadorans to eat well, to go to school, or to live decently. So few schools are provided by the government that not even half the citizens can read and write.

Until the problem of the guerrilla movement is solved, El Salvador will hardly be able to solve its problems of poverty, malnutrition, and education. The political decisions of the country affect the lives of all Salvadorans.

NICARAGUA

Sprawling across the middle of the Central American isthmus is the nation with the biggest area of all these small countries: the Republic of Nicaragua. In spite of its size—roughly the same as the state of Wisconsin—Nicaragua is the most thinly populated of the Central American countries, with about 2,500,000 people. Three-fourths of them live in one-fourth of the country's land, the low plain surrounding Nicaragua's two immense and unusual lakes, Nicaragua and Managua.

Long ago these big lakes were a bay of the Pacific Ocean, but erupting volcanoes spewed forth lava, setting up a land barrier and locking in this arm of the sea. Over hundreds of years the water in the lakes gradually became fresh, and just as gradually the saltwater fish became adapted to living in it. Today sharks, tarpon, and swordfish abound in these saltless waters—the only place in the world where this is true.

The largest of Lake Nicaragua's islands, Ometepe, has a two-headed volcano, one peak of which erupted some years ago. Hundreds of other islands, known as Las Isletas, dot the lake with their luxuriant green vegetation. Many of them are inhabited.

Out of Lake Nicaragua flows the San Juan River. It is broad and navigable and, more important to Nicaragua's history, it flows into the Caribbean Sea. Over the years the river, Lake Nicaragua, and the narrow, 12-mile (19.2-km) bar of land that separates the lake from the Pacific have made an easy natural route across Central America.

At the time of the Spaniards' arrival, a large number of Indians lived on the shores of Lake Nicaragua ("Nicarao's water"). And there, in 1522, the Indian chief Nicarao met the Spanish conqueror Gil González de Avila. The chief consented to be baptized a Catholic and issued orders for his tribe to do likewise.

A few years later colonists under Francisco Fernández de Córdoba arrived. (The country's money unit, the cordoba, is named for him.) On the shores of the two big lakes, Córdoba founded two cities—Granada on Lake Nicaragua and León on Lake Managua. Now the stage was set for Nicaragua's violent colonial history.

The wild Miskito Indians of the Caribbean coast crossed the isthmus to make occasional raids on the Pacific shore settlements. English, Dutch, and French pirates holed up in the protected bays along the Caribbean. From there they made forays into the Caribbean and attacked ships trading along the Spanish Main. One of the Caribbean ports, Bluefields, has a name taken from that of the Dutch pirate Blewfeldt. But the pirates' favorite port was Greytown (now called San Juan del Norte) at the mouth of the San Juan River. Most of the English pirates were based here. Up the San Juan passed the pirates Francis Drake and John Hawkins on their way to sack the proud city of Granada on Lake Nicaragua.

The English made early settlements in Bluefields and Greytown, and there were many bitter fights as the Spanish attempted to dislodge them. The famous British admiral Lord Nelson, when an officer in his twenties, was defeated in an attempt to lead a British naval expedition up the San Juan River. The British were not finally pried loose from Nicaragua until the latter half of the nineteenth century.

As if this were not enough discord in one country, the cities of Granada and León became great rivals. Granada was the center of commerce because of its key location on the water route across the isthmus. León was the seat of culture and learning and of the university. Playing on this rivalry, a North American adventurer, William Walker, won the support of the citizens of León in 1856 and made himself president of Nicaragua. He was soon ousted, however, when Central Americans of other countries took up arms and helped drive him from Nicaragua.

Another North American active in Nicaragua was Commodore Cornelius Vanderbilt. After the California gold rush started, in 1849, many Americans took the trip around Cape Horn to California. Vanderbilt hit on a shorter route: he operated river steamboats that took passengers from Greytown up the San Juan River and through Lake Nicaragua. There stagecoaches carried them across the narrow remaining strip of land to the Pacific Ocean, where they boarded ships to California. Vanderbilt's fee for an across-the-isthmus trip was fantastically high, but those who dreaded the months-long, storm-crossed voyage around the Horn willingly paid the price.

When the United States was considering digging a canal across Central America, Nicaraguans naturally urged that the canal be built along Vanderbilt's route. The Panama route won out, but during two world wars the United States considered making an additional canal in Nicaragua.

Managua, the capital of the country, is a city of more than 400,000 people located on the south shore of beautiful Lake Managua. It was largely destroyed by an earthquake in 1931, rebuilt and destroyed by another earthquake in 1972. After partial rebuilding and some relocation to the suburbs, it was severely damaged during the Civil War of 1978–79.

León, the second city of Nicaragua, was first founded on Lake

Managua but was moved to its present site away from the lake-shore after a volcanic eruption in 1609. It kept its classic Spanish colonial architecture, but it too suffered in the recent political strife.

The country is beginning to make a slow recovery from eighteen months of fighting, killing, and bombing between the army led by dictator Anastasio Somoza and the revolutionary guerrillas, called the "Sandinistas." The guerrillas took their name from Augusto Sandino, who had led an unsuccessful revolt many years before. At that time the first Anastasio Somoza (father of the recently ousted Somoza) seized the presidency and had Sandino put to death.

The two Somozas, first the father and then the son, ruled Nicaragua for a total of forty-two years without holding free elections. The Sandinistas won the support of the people, and after months of general strife, Anastasio Somoza, Jr., was forced to flee the country. The Sandinistas took control. A committee of nine persons, nearly all Marxist Socialists, is running the country.

Rebuilding the nation is a long and hard job. The Somoza family had controlled much of the country's wealth—its only cement factory, for example, in a country in which most of the new buildings are made of concrete. The Somozas also owned the country's airline. In fact, they had a controlling interest in the country's twenty-six largest companies. They also owned tremendous amounts of agricultural land—an area so large that it would be about the size of the country of El Salvador.

Basically Nicaragua is a rich country with many natural resources (mainly agricultural) and a small population. Now the country is suffering from inflation and unemployment. Also, because the new government is working closely with Fidel Castro's Communist representatives, private business from other countries is not eager to invest money in Nicaragua.

When the civil war began, Nicaragua's three chief export crops were coffee, cotton, and sugar. These were encouraged by United States technicians of the Agency for International Development (AID) as well as the United Nations after the leaf disease siga-

*Herds of cattle, such as these, have
become a less familiar sight in Nicaragua
since the Sandinistas revolution.*

toka destroyed Nicaragua's tremendous banana-raising industry.

The new Government of National Reconstruction (GNR) took over nearly half the farmland and has set goals for farm production in an Economic Reactivation Plan. However, many of the farm managers have left the country, and the new government has not been able to meet the goals of its plan.

Beef production and export were also important in Nicaragua until the revolution. Since then there has been a large reduction in dairy cows and beef cattle caused both by illegal cattle shipments to bordering countries and to too much butchering of cattle during and just after the revolution.

Coffee production has been reduced because of heavy rains and a shortage of workers to harvest the crop. Also a coffee rust disease has attacked the coffee trees in central Nicaragua, and the government has set up a project to destroy the trees with rust and to plant new young trees.

Before the revolution one of Nicaragua's important exports was gold. Mining was one of the first industries to be nationalized by the GNR, and gold production is now under government control.

Two Nicaraguan crafts came to a near standstill during the revolution and are expected to be in production again. One was the making of fine silver and gold filigree jewelry. The other was the production of hammocks, a craft that was centered in the little town of Masaya near the city of Managua.

One of Nicaragua's prime problems has been illiteracy. Nearly half the population over ten years of age is unable to read. In the years before the revolution, both the United States' AID program and the United Nations had worked to help reduce Nicaragua's illiteracy. Since the end of the civil war, Cuba has sent two thousand teachers to work in the country's schools.

In order for a country to have a good school system, good government is needed, and Nicaragua's has been unstable throughout its history. From 1912 to 1925, the United States Marines were in the country to help keep internal order. They returned again, but left permanently in 1933. Education progress was slow during the long Somoza government reign. It is too early to tell if the new GNR government will finally bring democratic rule and good educational opportunities to war-torn Nicaragua, or if a new kind of dictatorship is developing there.

COSTA RICA

Next to the smallest of the isthmian republics, Costa Rica is situated betweeen Nicaragua and Panama. It is a friendly land, often called the Switzerland of the Americas. Like Switzerland, Costa Rica is small and mountainous, with clean cities and progressive people. It does not maintain an army, and with a Civil Guard force of a few thousand, it boasts that it has more schoolteachers than soldiers. Its schools are some of the finest in Latin America, and nine-tenths of the population can read, the highest literacy rate in Central America.

For a Latin American country, Costa Rica is unusual in that it was truly colonized and not divided for spoils. In 1562, Governor Juan Vasquez de Coronado brought about fifty families from the Basque region and the Spanish provinces of Galicia and Aragon to Costa Rica's rich central highlands. Their aim was not to return to Spain after grabbing big tracts of land, but to stay and make Costa Rica their home. With few exceptions the country was divided into small farms from the very start, and many of these properties have stayed in the same families since the beginning.

After the coming of the Spanish, the Indian population decreased quickly until it was almost nothing. And since Costa Rica was considered too hilly for big plantations that might require Negro slaves, none was imported. As a result, the Costa Ricans today are mostly Spanish in ancestry; many of them have the blue eyes of their forebears. Costa Rican men call one another "Brother." Since a large part of the population is descended from those fifty families, it is likely that they are at least distant cousins.

Like other Central American countries, Costa Rica supports itself mainly by agriculture. Bananas are the big crop of the low-

lands, and coffee of the highlands. In addition to these export crops, beef, cacao, and sugar are also important; and corn, tobacco, rice, beans, and potatoes are grown for home consumption. Costa Rica is unlike some of its neighbors, however, in that it does not suffer from absentee landowners and their lack of interest.

The increase in world oil prices in the late 1970s has fueled the inflation in Costa Rica, which must import all its oil. In 1980 it spent as much money on oil as it made on coffee, its chief export crop. The drop in coffee prices has also been hard on Costa Rica, which is having a difficult time paying off heavy debts.

San José, the capital of the country, is on the coffee-growing central plateau. It is a sparkling-white city of 250,000 people, pleasant and peaceful, with a beautiful National Theater and a National Museum that contains a fine collection of ancient Indian handiwork. The city's altitude of 3,814 feet (1,144 m) results in a pleasant year-round temperature of from 55 to 80°F (12.7 to 26.6°C). From the air above it, two oceans can be seen, yet it is not a seaport.

In 1964 a law was passed giving special privileges to foreigners who wish to retire in Costa Rica. Several hundred people, mostly from the United States, have since settled in the city of San José and have been warmly welcomed by the Costa Ricans. A railroad joins San José with Puntarenas, on the Pacific coast, and with Limón, on the Caribbean, thus giving the capital a port on each ocean. There is also a rather new highway between San José and Limón.

Formerly the capital of the country, Cartago, 14 miles (22.4 km) from San José, is a historic spot. The shrine of Our Lady of the Angels, the patron saint of Costa Rica, is there. Her feast day, August 2, is celebrated throughout the country as a national holi-

This ceramic monkey-effigy vessel, made before A.D. 300, can be seen at the National Museum in San José.

*Beautiful scenery surrounds this Costa Rican factory
at Golfito, which makes edible vegetable oil products.*

day. In Cartago also are the College of San Luis Gonzaga, and the Hospital Maximiliano Peralta, named for one of Costa Rica's great doctors.

The Inter-American Highway runs the length of Costa Rica, climbing over 10,000 feet (3,000 m) high at some points. Transportation is good on the central plateau, and additional roads have been built in the less populated parts of the country.

Loans from the World Bank are helping Costa Rica to build a new hydroelectric plant and to improve the water mains in the city of San José.

On the back roads of the plateau, genuine Costa Rican oxcarts can still be seen. Local farmers take a tremendous pride in these beautifully painted wagons and they decorate each one individually. Because their owners wish the cartwheels to "sing," cartmakers select carefully seasoned wood, which, for each wheel, they cut into sixteen pie-shaped wedges. These are then fitted into an iron tire, and the resulting wheel is adjusted on the axle of a cart in such a way as to make a resonant, rattling sound, pleasant to the ear of the cart owner.

Costa Rica has some famous sights. One is the popular bathing resort called Ojo de Agua, Spanish for "eye of the water." It is a lavish mountain spring from which water flows at the rate of 6,000 gallons (22,800 l) a minute. Besides furnishing water for the city of Puntarenas, it has an overflow that supplies a huge swimming pool.

Another sight of the country is the famous Poás Volcano, high in the mountains. Its crater, one of the largest in the world, formerly had one of the largest geysers as well. Some years ago, Poás swallowed its water, however, and now is an ordinary smoking volcano.

PANAMA

The southernmost country on the land bridge between North and South America was not part of the original federation of Central American republics. Panama, which occupies the very narrowest part of the isthmus between North and South America, was a province of the South American country now called Colombia, until gaining independence early in this century.

Even now, some Panamanians prefer to think of themselves as South Americans, although the country holds membership in a number of Central American regional groups.

Almost since Vasco Núñez de Balboa crossed Panama to reach the Pacific Ocean, people have been traveling across this narrow place between the oceans. Fewer than thirty years after Columbus discovered America, the Spanish built the cobblestone *Camino Real* (kah-MEE-no ray-AHL), the Royal Road. Over this highway the gold and silver of Peru, brought by ship to the Pacific coast city of Panama, moved by well-guarded donkey carts to the Atlantic coast. There, other Spanish ships, moving on a well-arranged schedule, waited to take the valuable plunder to Spain.

The Panama–Costa Rican border cuts through the mountain range that divides the two republics. The highlands of the Chiriqui border province make the country's best coffee-producing land, and coffee *fincas* (FEEN-kas) or farms, are scattered throughout the area. Raising beef cattle is a major industry here. On both the Caribbean and Pacific coasts, close to the Costa Rican border, large American-owned banana plantations employ hundreds of Panamanians.

Eastward from Costa Rica, the Caribbean coast of Panama is mountainous for most of its length to the Panama Canal and very sparsely populated. But on the Pacific side the mountains give way to *llanos* (LYAH-nos) or plains. These central plains are the dairy region of Panama. Some of the best milk-producing cattle here are a cross between the humped Brahman cows of India and dairy breeds such as the Jersey. Like their Indian ancestors, these cows can withstand tremendous heat, and like their Jersey ancestors, they are good milk producers.

Sugar cane is also grown in this savannah region, and is processed into both brown and white sugar.

Going east from the *llanos* region, the land slopes down to the narrowest, lowest part of the isthmus, once treacherous fever country. Here, in the nineteenth century, the French tried unsuc-

*Plantation workers make ready
to cut a stem of bananas.*

cessfully to dig a canal. They were defeated by the unforeseen hardships and great expense of the job. As much as anything else, they quit because of the terrible death toll from yellow fever and malaria in these swampy lowlands.

A decade later, sparked by the enthusiasm of young President Theodore Roosevelt, the United States began to dig a canal where the French had failed.

Two major changes helped the Americans succeed. Panama, which had been a province of Colombia, revolted with American help and declared its independence (two previous revolts had failed). Second, army doctor Walter Reed and his team had discovered in Cuba during the Spanish-American War that mosquitoes caused yellow fever and malaria.

Science and public health practices kept the Americans' work force healthy. Army engineers assigned to the job solved the engineering, geological, and construction problems. And in 1914, the modern construction miracle the Panama Canal opened to the ships of the world.

Under the terms of a treaty with Panama, the Panama Canal Zone was created, under which Panama ceded to the United States "in perpetuity," which means forever, certain lands surrounding the area in which the canal was to be dug.

The Canal Zone, in which thousands of Americans eventually lived, operating, maintaining, and protecting the Panama Canal, was abolished in 1979. Under new treaties most of the land of the Zone went to Panama. A narrow frame of land surrounding the canal, as well as other defense areas, will be ceded to Panama on an elaborate timetable that goes until the year 2000, when Panama itself will take possession of the Panama Canal.

East of the canal and south to the Colombian border lies a kind of no-man's-land—the province of Darién, where two distinct Indian tribes—the Cunas and the Chocós—still maintain a local independence in the jungles as well as on the hundreds of little Caribbean islands, the San Blas Archipelago.

Wild game still abounds in the jungles, and some foresting of mahogany trees takes place in Darién. The Inter-American High-

*A Japanese container ship is eased
into the Pedro Miguel locks on its
northbound transit of the Panama Canal.*

way, which goes all through Central America, comes to an end some 50 miles (80 km) east of the Panama Canal near the town of Yaviza. People who want to drive on to South America must leave the road before the Darién Gap, as it is called, and take the car by ship from the Panama Canal to the port of Cartagena, Colombia. There they can pick up the highway again.

Panama City is the capital of the republic. With a population of nearly a half million, it is a modern and progressive city with fine hotels, two universities, and beautiful residential areas as well as low-cost housing areas.

Tourism is a major industry, largely because of the constant stream of visitors to the Panama Canal. A new convention center is expected to attract group meetings to the city from other countries.

Panama has one of the highest literacy rates among the Central American countries. It spends more than 21 percent of its government budget for education, more than for anything else. The University of Panama, which was founded in 1935, has both law and medical schools and recently opened a school of dentistry. These educational opportunities are helping in the increase in the middle class as the education level of the country rises.

Panama's four major exports are bananas, refined petroleum products (from imported oil at an Atlantic side refinery), shrimp, and sugar.

BELIZE

On September 21, 1981, the last colonial ties in Central America were broken when the former colony of British Honduras became the new country of Belize, politically independent of Great Britain. Actually, Belize had enjoyed parliamentary self-government since 1964, but a longtime dispute with Guatemala delayed independence. The dispute was finally settled in the United Nations in 1979 with the help of Mexico and Panama, and Central America gained another country.

Belize is very small, the size of Massachusetts, with a population of only about 150,000. English is the official language, although Spanish is spoken widely. The people of Belize have more in common with the other English-speaking people of the Caribbean islands than with Central Americans of Spanish-Indian origin. Their ancestors were English woodcutters and black slaves, the original immigrants to the area. In English colonial days Belize was a good source of Honduran mahogany, much prized for making fine furniture. The city of Belize (population 40,000) was established by the British in the seventeenth century as the capital of a colony established on land that the Spanish claimed but did not settle.

Belize City was built on the edge of a mangrove swamp just 18 inches (45.7 cm) above sea level, a perfect location to be hit by hurricanes. In this century two have struck the city within forty years.

After Hurricane Hattie hit and did extensive damage in 1961, the British moved the capital 60 miles (96 km) inland. They created a new little village at the base of the small country's mountain range and named it Belmopan. New government buildings were erected, as well as housing for the government employees. So far the little village has not grown much, but the hope is that it will become a much larger community.

Beyond the swampy seacoast, which has no beaches but has the world's second-longest barrier reef, lies the jungle. In recent years the valuable mahogany supply has begun to dwindle. Sugar has become the principal export, and efforts are being made to increase the production of rice, beef, bananas, and other tropical fruit for export as well as citrus fruits, lobster, and fish.

Belize has some 2 million acres (.8 million ha) of land that could be used for farming. At this time only a fraction of it is planted.

In its new role as a parliamentary democracy, like many Commonwealth nations, Belize will have Queen Elizabeth II as its head of state. George Price, who had been premier since Belize became self-governing in 1964, moved in 1981 to the position of first prime minister and foreign minister.

*Modern harvesting equipment helps
increase the production of rice.*

Great Britain and the United States are both contributing to helping the little country in its new role for the next few years. By then the United Nations and the International Monetary Fund, which Belize plans to join, will probably be able to extend benefits to this new member.

As soon as Belize achieved its independence, in October of 1981, Guatemala closed the gate at the border town of San Ignacio on the only highway connecting the country with Belize. Persons from Belize are not permitted to enter or leave Guatemala. However, international travelers on this poor road from the Mayan ruins of Tikal in Guatemala to Belize's capital at Belmopan are allowed to pass through.

How the Central Americans Live

On the Central American isthmus live about 22 million people, mostly of the Roman Catholic faith and whose official language is Spanish. The exception is the newly independent Belize, where English is spoken and the most common religion is Protestant Christianity.

Traditionally, the Central American people have tended to stay put. Many families, rich and poor alike, have not moved 20 miles (32 km) in a period of three or four hundred years. As a result, in one particular village there may be two hundred or more people with the same family name. Many of the townspeople are cousins and often look alike.

Central American families are very close. They are loyal to their family members and seek few friends outside the family circle. Often they are hardly conscious of their neighbors, unless they are also relatives. Grandparents are highly respected as the leaders of the group. When a son of the family marries, he often brings his wife home with him. Then everyone helps build a house—or a hut—for him on the family land, if there is any.

A child's birthday party does not necessarily mean a party for a group of school or neighborhood youngsters the age of the child, as would be the American custom. Instead, a birthday is an occasion for a family reunion, with relatives of all ages from the oldest down to the newest baby cousin.

Social and political events in the past decade have changed this tradition of family closeness in many areas. For example, the lure of the cities is breaking up families in small villages and on farms. As education has improved in Central America, most of the new high schools and vocational schools have been built in the cities. Also, job opportunities have developed in the cities. Cities are where the radio and television stations are located. All of these things have combined to attract many *campesinos* to move from the farms to the cities. At the fringes of the cities are shack towns, hovels made of pieces of wood, tin, plastic, and cardboard that the poorest people live in while they seek education for their children, work for themselves, and try to fit into big town life. In Panama the shacks are called *casas brujas* (KAH-sas BROO-has) or "witches' houses," because they seem to appear overnight out of nowhere.

The older houses of the wealthy Central Americans are often much like the traditional houses of Spain. The outside is usually very plain and built right up to the sidewalk or street. There is no particular decoration for the benefit of passersby, except often a very beautiful door knocker and ornate wrought iron across the windows and doors.

When the big, heavy door opens and a Central American invites guests to enter, they step into a vestibule with a ceramic tile floor. In contrast with the plain outside, the walls and floors may be decorated with patterns of brightly patterned tile. Moving from the entry into other rooms, many guests are surprised to find that the house is built around a garden. This garden, or patio, is surrounded by a *corredor* (COR-ray-DOR), or covered walk, onto which all the rooms open, sometimes from two floors.

A person getting up in the morning looks—not out the window but inward toward the *corredor*, to see the house's private yard or garden (sometimes with a lily pond or fountain in the center).

A colonial-style patio, surrounded by a corredor

An Indian adobe hut in the highlands

Many of the newer homes are being built without an enclosed patio, more in the "California" style of architecture. But many Central Americans still prefer to have their gardens where the family, not the passersby, can enjoy them.

But only the wealthy people can afford homes of this kind. All through Central America a majority of the people live in poor ramshackle huts. At sea level these are made of palm fronds. In the drier climate of the highlands, adobe—mud and brick—is sometimes used. In some of the countries, United States AID programs have taught people to make concrete blocks so that they can build their own cement homes.

Since traditionally most of the land has belonged to the rich, some people live as squatters. They put up a small house almost anywhere in the countryside and live there until the owner drives them off.

The political unrest in Central America has made the housing shortage even greater. Some of Nicaragua's housing was destroyed in the recent revolution. Terrorist activities in El Salvador have added to the homeless refugee problem and have discouraged homebuilding. Even in politically stable Costa Rica, the inflation problem means fewer homes are being built.

Children in Central America generally attend school in the rainy season (*invierno* or winter) and have vacation in the dry season (*verano* or summer). The school year varies slightly from country to country. In Guatemala and El Salvador, vacation is from the end of October to early in January. Nearer the equator, in Panama, vacation runs from January to May. But all Central American schoolchildren attend classes in May, June, July, August, and September, when it rains in all the countries. Most of the public schools are coeducational, with boys and girls in the same classroom. However, most Catholic schools, mainly in the larger towns and cities, still have separate schools for boys and girls.

In their free time the children at the hot seacoasts enjoy playing at the beaches and climbing palm trees for coconuts. They like to hack off a piece of *caña* (KAH-nya) or sugar cane, with a sharp machete and suck it for the juice. Those who live in the *tierra templada*—the highlands—sometimes ride horses or burros, help pick the coffee beans on the coffee *fincas,* or sort out oranges for market.

Many homes have television sets and most have radios.

Girls in Central America stay at home much more than they do in North America. It is not considered good manners for them to go anywhere alone. And for boys and girls in their teens to go out by themselves on a date in the North American way would not be thought proper. Only in recent years have women begun to attend colleges and study for careers. In Panama, which has had the most outside influence, there are several women in government and the professions: there are women lawyers, doctors, dentists, and several prominent educators. The Central American universities are gradually improving, and women are allowed to enroll. Life is changing in Central America, although to some the changes are coming slowly.

Traveling through Central America

The first railroad built in Central America ran across Panama from the Caribbean to the Pacific. This first transcontinental railroad was completed in 1855. Later, a British-built railroad ran across Nicaragua from coast to coast. The United Fruit Company eventually built several railroads, most of them at sea level, to haul bananas to port. The Mexico-to-Panama railroad got only as far as Guatemala; building railroads through the mountains cost too much, and the risks involved were too great for any investor. There were many attempts to join Central America by rail started in many places, but this dream was never realized.

It was the commercial airlines that first linked Central America from Panama to Mexico and opened up the mountainous, roadless isthmus to the outside world. Air transportation is still the most important means of international passenger movement in Central America and Panama.

In 1929 Charles A. Lindbergh piloted a Sikorsky S-38 flying boat 3,000 miles (4,800 km) to open a new mail route to Panama. The history-making experiment took three days. He flew, with frequent refueling stops, from Dinner Key, in Florida, to western Cuba, then on to Honduras, Nicaragua, and at last to Panama. Following this flight, Pan American Airways began regular commercial flights through Central America.

Its best-known flight was the one from Mexico City to Panama City and back again, through the capitals of all the Central American republics. Central American residents from the United States called it "the milk run." As a slow train in the United States used to stop at little towns to pick up cans of milk, so the airline "milk run" would stop in each small republic, connecting six countries in a way the railroad builders never dreamed possible.

The "milk run" flight stopped running after many years, when each of the Central American republics had at last established its own small airline. Now several airlines—at least one from each Central American country—connect the republics. Flights from some of the small countries also go to Los Angeles, Mexico City, New Orleans, and Miami. Civil aviation has grown fast in Central America. Within these countries little local airlines also make regular runs in small aircraft for short distances that would be traveled by car in a country with a good road system.

Pan American no longer flies through Central America. Its planes travel from Miami to Panama, where connections can be made for many parts of South America. Panama City's airport is larger and busier than any of the others in Central America, for at Panama air routes come together from many points. It is the last stopping place before the leap to the landmass of South America.

In 1930, the same year Pan American Airways began to fly through Central America, the United States began to help the six republics build the Inter-American Highway. This ambitious project goes from Texas to Panama City. The United States paid for two-thirds of the road and loaned money to the other countries for their share of the expense. Building the highway was a long and discouraging job. It runs 3,150 miles (5,035.6 km) through some of the world's densest jungle and zigzags over mountains previously uncharted. Hundreds of expensive bridges were needed to span a myriad of little rivers.

*The lack of a good road system means a frequent
use of small aircraft in Central America.*

Each of two streams on the route is referred to as "the great river of trouble" in the country where it brings floods and destruction. One stream is the Río Selegua in Guatemala; the other is the Río Grande de Térraba in Costa Rica. Both gave the highway builders tremendous problems to solve.

In Guatemala all the experience and skills of the United States contractors were needed to bulldoze through Selegua Canyon. Deep cuts had to be made in the canyon walls. Then, in the rainy season, came the slides. To remove them and to prevent further slides, many more thousands of tons of earth had to be moved than had been allowed for in the original contracts.

In Costa Rica the rugged land along the Rio Grande made trouble. The line of the road had to be changed constantly as the contractors' machines unearthed unsuitable materials.

Now the highway is paved concrete from Guatemala to the Panama Canal. From one end to the other, little signs with the numeral "1" mark this first international highway through Central America.

Along the whole route the landslides have been more frequent, the rains heavier, the soil more difficult, the forest more dense than in road building elsewhere. These difficulties slowed down by years the finishing of the road. For the same reasons it is a difficult highway to maintain. Responsibility for maintaining the road belongs to each republic the road goes through.

The bridges were among the biggest stumbling blocks to finishing the highway. Driving over one of these bridges during the dry season, a person looks down and sees a tiny trickle of water far below. The bridge looks like a great waste of cement—a concrete monster on broad bastions, crouching over a nearly dry stream bed. But the rains of August and September change the trickle into a wild, roaring torrent, rushing under the bridge, carrying whole tree trunks along with it. Suddenly, the bridge looks too small to withstand the tremendous flood force.

Connecting the countries from the United States to the Panama Canal, the road is a tremendous step forward in bringing all North and Central Americans closer together.

However, terrorist activities in Central America beginning in the mid-1970s and continuing into the 1980s have often discouraged use of the Inter-American Highway. Roadblocks have been set up by terrorists of the Sandinistas and the rightist groups at various times in some of the countries. While Nicaragua's civil war took place in the late 1970s, few people dared to drive through the country.

The trouble in El Salvador can be avoided if a driver coming south from Guatemala on the Inter-American Highway turns eastward to Guatemala City. By taking another road into northeastern Guatemala, one can proceed into Honduras and never pass through El Salvador at all. At the capital city of Tegucigalpa, the driver can head south over a new road and join the Inter-American Highway again near the Pacific coast.

Soon the Nicaraguan border approaches. Highway No. 1 runs directly through Nicaragua near the Pacific coast, going outside the cities of Cinandega, León, and Managua, which were severely damaged by the 1972 earthquake and recently by the revolution. In five hours of driving one arrives at the Costa Rican border. There is no fear of roadblocks in this peaceful country (which has no military force) or in Panama beyond.

In spite of earthquakes, Nicaragua's revolution, and terrorist activities in several countries, the Inter-American Highway is still complete and usable. The driver should beware of potholes, herds of cattle, or a passing snake in the early morning. But the Inter-American Highway is an engineering feat, completed after years of dreams and hopes and very hard construction work. Both Central and North Americans can continue to take pride in it.

Before the highway was built through Central America, the only way to reach many towns was by trail. In dry season people went by horse. When the trail became so wet that the horse's broad hooves stuck in the mud, the Central American traveler used a mule, which has a smaller hoof. When the rains made the trail too muddy for the mule, a bull cart was used. A bull has a cleft hoof that does not stick, because the mud goes right through the cleft. If the trail became so muddy that the cart would not go through, the owner rode on the bull's back. When the mud was so

A newly cut road through the jungle

thick that even the bull could not get through the trail, the Central American stayed at home.

Many isolated villages of Central America had remained almost unchanged since Spanish colonial times. Now, wherever new highways have touched, a new life has begun. A little village like Santo Tomás, in Nicaragua, is an example. Formerly, this village could be reached from the city of Managua only by taking an hour's trip overland and a three-hour boat ride across Lake Nicaragua, then undertaking a tedious four-hour trek by packhorse over a jungle trail. Any mail or machinery had to go to Santo Tomás the same way. Anyone who bothered to make the trip found Santo Tomás a beautiful little town with orange trees growing in every yard and along all the streets. There were so many oranges—with no place to market them—that they sold for the equivalent of a penny each.

Then the United States built the Rama Road from coast to coast, branching off the Inter-American Highway and passing through Santo Tomás. Now mail and materials arrive by highway from Managua in only half an hour. The townspeople can easily move their fruit to market, and the price of oranges has risen to five cents each. At last, and with a suddenness that is hard to believe, Santo Tomás has come into the twentieth century.

This has happened in hundreds of towns along the Inter-American Highway. Travel on the road far exceeds the most optimistic estimates of highway engineers. Moreover, Central American countries have been quick to build feeder roads to connect other cities to the highway.

Many bus routes over the highway make it possible for people to travel cheaply to any Central American country, except when guerrilla activity interferes in El Salvador, Guatemala, or Honduras.

Another equally ambitious project is to connect the Inter-American Highway with the Pan-American Highway that goes through South America. The big problem is the dense jungle and swampy areas of Panama's Darién Province. About 100 miles (160 km), including 30 miles (48 km) of swamp, now constitute the Darién Gap.

The United States funded construction in Panama of the road from the Panama Canal almost to the town of Yavisa. In Colombia, U.S. funds paid to move the Pan-American Highway northward. Colombia paid for the last 3 miles (4.8 km) to the edge of the great swamp.

Now Colombia has proposed a new and cheaper way to connect the Central and South American highways. It proposes, as a short-term solution, to dig a canal through the swamp rather than build a highway. Automobiles and trucks would then be ferried across the canal, and a most difficult part of the highway construction could be avoided. However, funds for the canal have not been forthcoming from Colombia.

Another difficult situation has arisen that now discourages connecting the two highways after all. South American countries continue to have a great problem with hoof and mouth disease, a highly contagious illness that strikes and destroys whole herds of cattle. Central and North American cattle have not yet been touched by this disease. Cattle owners from Panama all the way north to Texas fear what would happen if the two highways were joined. Trucks carrying disease-bearing cattle might cross frontiers in spite of the best intentions of border guards. The disease could move northward very quickly.

Until vaccines completely eliminate the hoof and mouth disease problem, many people in several countries feel that money should not be spent to join the two roads. Connecting all the Americas, they feel, must await further scientific research in laboratories and work among cattle herds to eradicate this terrible disease or to provide complete immunity from it.

The Future of
Central America

Every country on the Central American isthmus except Costa Rica has had a history of violence and revolution and unstable governments. Never has the violence been so great, so present in nearly every country as in the late 1970s and early 1980s. Never has the future of Central America looked so bleak.

Dependence on very few export crops helped to make these countries sensitive to political turmoil. In the seventeenth century that export crop was cacao; in the eighteenth it was indigo; in the late nineteenth and twentieth centuries, bananas have been a particularly important export. United States interests have owned the banana crops and have influenced the politics. From this history came the term "banana republic," which means any one-crop country with an unstable government.

In most of the countries a small, white, upper-class group with roots back to the Spanish colonists owned most of the land, intermarried, and in that way kept the money and the power and the pure Spanish blood within a small group. In Panama this group is called the *rabiblancos* (RAH-bee-BLAN-kos), that is "the white-tails."

Almost two-thirds of the people of Central America are rural peasants, of mixed Spanish and Indian blood, working on farms or plantations owned by a few wealthy families or a foreign controlled corporation.

The rate of illiteracy is very high in Central America. More than 80 percent of the Indians in Guatemala do not read. In fact, a large percentage speak no Spanish—only the Indian tongue of their Maya ancestors.

With a history of frequent revolutions and unstable government, of little money spent on education and of land ownership confined to a few, democratic government has little chance to grow.

In the 1950s and 1960s the United States poured millions and millions of dollars into Central America and Panama to encourage development of industry, agriculture, health, roads, and community development. Without democratic government in these countries, in some ways the Point Four and AID money made the rich richer and the poor poorer. When Somoza was finally overthrown in 1979, for example, the Somoza family fortune was $500 million, while the average Nicaraguan's annual income was $660.

In the long, violent history of Central America, leaders of the Catholic Church would avoid politics and generally go along with the government in power. However, this situation changed in the late 1960s when priests and religious helpers educated in "liberation theology" began working with the poor. They believe that the "social sins" of poverty, exploitation, and political repression must be corrected.

Rather than encouraging the poor to continue to accept their lot, the newly trained clergy and religious urged the poor to demand rights, such as seeking land reform—dividing up large estates to give poor peasants land. Some priests and sisters started cooperatives for the poor—making it possible for them to sell their farm products as a group to make more profit and to buy things as a group to get lower prices.

Many people in power—landowners, businessmen, and others of the far right—did not agree with the new role of priests and religious and the movements they were developing. Since 1977, twenty-four priests and three nuns, both natives and missionaries from other countries, have been murdered in Central America for working with the poor or supporting them in ways those in power wanted stopped. These unsolved murders may have been committed by security forces of the governments in power, others possibly by leftist revolutionaries.

In 1982 in El Salvador and Guatemala, at last land reforms have begun. The big plantation owners are sharing their land with the thousands of rural poor who have none. This movement, started by former president José Napoleón Duarte in El Salvador, may improve the lot of his country's poor, undernourished, undereducated peasants.

However, leaders who now try to put Central American countries on a new, democratic course may be too late. The leftist guerrillas do not want peaceful solutions. They continue to raid, to bomb, and to kill to keep the countries in a state of turmoil. In El Salvador, they remain entrenched in isolated parts of Morazán and Chalatenango provinces near the Honduran border, where they can maintain external supply lines.

The leftists have the support of Fidel Castro's Communists in nearby Cuba, who are working to export their leftist government to other Caribbean islands and to Central America as well.

Cuban leftists fought in Nicaragua alongside the Nicaraguan Sandinistas to win that revolution. Now, with a primarily Marxist council running Nicaragua, Cuban guerrillas have moved into El Salvador. Revolutionaries from as far away as East Germany and Vietnam have joined the guerrillas to keep up the violence there. They have even brought in American-made guns and mortars that U.S. forces left in Vietnam.

Some foreign affairs experts see the "domino" theory in Central America's future. If El Salvador follows Nicaragua into Communist hands, next to fall would be Guatemala. Then Honduras would go. Panama, where U.S. troops still guard the Panama Canal, would fall last, along with peaceful Costa Rica.

Any government that survives in Central America will face a future with many problems, as the Nicaraguan leftists are now discovering. If land reform succeeds, or if the leftists win in other countries and the land is turned into government-owned collectives as in Nicaragua, severe problems remain.

In Central America almost no work has been done in the conservation of soil and water resources. Although in the dry season the land lies cracked and dry and dusty, during the rainy season the water rushes into both oceans with a fantastic roar. Each year hundreds of tons of fertile soil drain off into the ocean, leaving the land a little more parched, a little less rich. Work is being done to help to conserve some of that water during the rainy season.

In some areas, irrigation is necessary in the dry season. AID experts taught farmers how to irrigate their land in the simplest, cheapest fashion in order that the poorest farmers as well as the large landowners could be helped. With AID help, thousands of communities were supplied with potable water. AID grants for materials helped build reservoirs and dig wells. But other thousands of Central American farms still have no running water.

Forest conservation practices must also be taught. The jungles of Central America are gradually losing their fine stands of mahogany, sapodilla, and other woods; any forward-looking program should include replanting the tropical hardwoods.

A successful development in Central America is the raising of the African oil palm, which in past decades has been introduced into Honduras, Nicaragua, Panama, and Costa Rica. Five years after planting, this tree produces fruit that furnishes a great quantity of vegetable oil for cooking and for making margarine and soap. Its widespread cultivation has already been successful in Costa Rica and Panama. United Brand's tropical agriculturalists recently developed soybean seed for tropical cultivation. Soybeans can be an important source of edible oil, a food product in short supply in Central America.

Cattle raising is one of the area's profitable industries. With the aid of United States experts, fine breeds of cattle were brought in, and milk and beef production have been increased. In the hot lands at sea level, breeds that can stand tropical heat have been

*It requires two workers to carry
the fruit of the African oil palm.*

introduced. AID experts in Panama introduced pangola grass for grazing cattle. It is quick-growing, produces a large tonnage of grass for each acre, and does not suffer from tropical plant diseases. Ranchers were taught the value of stock ponds, and wells were dug to furnish water for cattle during the dry season.

Many tourists from the United States, Canada, and Europe had discovered the beauties of the Central American countries when the growth of violence discouraged them from more visiting. Americans, Canadians, and Mexicans who had encouraged the construction of the Inter-American Highway were beginning to drive all the way down to Panama when the violence in Nicaragua stopped the travel. When the Nicaraguan revolution was over, increased trouble in Guatemala and El Salvador prevented much growth in the tourist business. Many hotels are empty, particularly in Guatemala, which had developed a brisk tourist business.

If and when peace arrives, the Central American countries will need international funding to continue industrial and agricultural growth. New harbors and airports, hydroelectric and geothermal plants, roads, and housing are all needed. To develop Central America's resources will take money. Perhaps the World Bank, the Inter-American Development Bank, and the International Monetary Fund will help to make these projects possible. But before much long-range planning can begin, Central America needs peace. Until then, the unfortunate peoples of these small republics face difficult times and little hope for brighter days.

Index